COLORS OF

Britain

AA Publishing

Author: Dr. Bernard Stonehouse

Produced by AA Publishing

Text © Automobile Association Developments Limited 2004
Reprinted 2006

Published by AA Publishing (a trading name of Automobile Association Developments Limited, whose registered office is Fanum House, Basing View, Basingstoke, Hampshire RG21 4EA; registered number 1878835).

ISBN-10: 0-7495-4236-5
ISBN-13: 978-0-7495-4236-8

A03193

A CIP catalogue record for this book is available from the British Library.

Printed and bound in China

COLORS OF

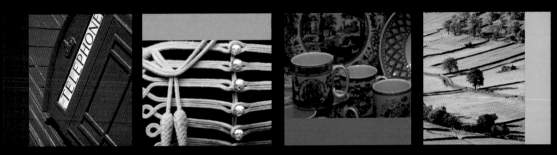

Britain

CON

1 FLAVORS

2 LIFE & PEOPLE

3 ARCHITECTURE

ENTS

COLORS OF **BRITAIN**

book is about. Britain is indeed colorful, and gets more so every day. Not in the brilliant, sun-burnished way of Italy, Greece, or Spain: Britain's natural palette is muted and restrained, as befits a cool temperate climate. It was indeed subdued by almost palpable haze for two centuries and more, when coal was king, and domestic and industrial smoke dimmed cities and countryside alike. But from the mid-20th century onward the decline in heavy industry and the increase in Clean Air Acts and availability of cheap electricity have worked together to clear the atmosphere. When the rain washed Britain clean, it showed up forgotten color in every corner of the realm.

That was half the story. The other half was a revolution in favor of man-made color that began over 50 years ago, bringing more varied and brighter shades into everyday life. Some may remember that a brighter-Britain campaign began with the 1951 Festival of Britain, when war-weary Brits broke free of constraints to welcome a new, brash wave of creativity. Buildings, furnishings, fabrics, clothes, toys, street signs all got the treatment: color came in wherever there was room for it. No more institution walls painted custard and brown. No more dark, chocolate-colored furniture. No more gray flannel trousers. Color quite simply became part of the scene. You don't go far in Britain today without seeing it, some still gentle and restrained, some scruffy and tatty, but plenty that is gaudy, cheerful, and compelling.

From Tribes to Great Britain

Roman Britannia was a predominantly green land, heavily forested with deciduous trees in the south and conifers in the colder north. It turned white overall, at least on the uplands, for two or three months every winter. A human population, perhaps numbering a few hundred thousand, perhaps a million or two, was already making inroads into the forest, clearing timber for fuel and to make way for crops. Brighter shades were probably rare. Ancient Britons, it is said, painted themselves with woad, a blue vegetable pigment, to impress their neighbors, and both natives and Romans used natural dyes and ground-rock pigments on a very limited scale to color fabrics, glass, and ceramics.

When the Romans left, other invaders quickly moved in. Crossing the North Sea in coracles (small, wicker-framed boats), galleys, and longboats, they found hospitable shores, navigable rivers

In Britain it's an institution, which the British call 'Tea' (above left); it happens around 4 o'clock in the afternoon and *everything* stops (or used to stop) for it. The basis is a pot of tea, freshly made in a teapot (that is important) with *boiling* water (even more important), and served either with milk

(and optional sugar) or with thinly sliced lemon. Enjoy this traditional Cornish tea, with scones (small plain cakes), clotted cream, and strawberry jam (jelly).

Thatched cottages such as these in the pretty village of Hinton St. George in Somerset (above) are to be found across the length and breadth of England.

winding far into fertile, underpopulated hinterlands, and a mild climate free from harsh central European winters. The newcomers—Frisians, Angles, Saxons, Jutes, and later the dreaded Vikings—continued clearing the forests, the demand for charcoal to fuel the iron industry in particular making huge inroads. Anglo-Saxon fields and grazing grounds formed patterns on the land that can still be traced today. Their patchwork of small, constantly warring kingdoms fell easy prey to the better-organized Normans from France. The Norman take-over from 1066 created order of a kind, distinguishing an English nation in the south from the less-tractable Welsh and Scots. At the Domesday survey of 1086 (a record of all lands in England), the country was revealed as a predominantly rural land of farms, forest, moorland, villages, and townships, with a population still around the one million mark.

England, Wales, and Scotland were separately identified, but Britannia was not yet Britain. That concept took a further five centuries to develop, bolstered by the steadily increasing prosperity of England, and the dominance of successive English kings. Wales was assimilated in 1536, to be ruled nominally by the English crown prince. 'Great Britain' made its official debut in 1604, when King James VI of Scotland, who had recently become James I of England, dubbed himself the first king of Great Britain.

United but Distinctive

So Britain today is a well-defined geographical location, and home to a well-defined British nation? Well, not quite. The three prototypic British nations, English, Scots, and Welsh, are all still very much in evidence. Visitors puzzle over the basic similarities yet deeply cherished differences manifest in accent, style, education, and ways of life. Far from diminishing, these differences are becoming more pronounced, most recently by devolution toward self-government.

There are profound differences between English and Scottish law, significant differences in education systems, and minor but entertaining differences in culture. The Welsh sing in male-voice choirs, the English in mixed-gender choral societies (except in the more traditional churches, where men and boys are the rule). Scots march to pipe bands, the English to brass bands. At traditional country gatherings the Welsh sing and recite poetry, the Scots dance and toss cabers (not unlike telegraph poles), and the English pin prize rosettes on horses, sheep, cattle, cakes, and jars of preserves. Though English is the common language, there are local dialects that, in their extreme forms, are mutually incomprehensible. Highland Scots and Welsh cherish quite different languages of their own.

Within the three nations there are finer, near-tribal distinctions. Highland Scots claim significant differences from lowland Scots, Yorkshire people from Lancastrians, the Cornish from Devonians,

People take to the streets for the Notting Hill Carnival at the end of August every year. This multicultural event is now the biggest street carnival in Europe and whole streets in the Notting Hill area of London are closed to traffic to accommodate the revellers.

London Cockneys from Newcastle Geordies. How different? How important are the differences? Go ask in the pubs: they'll be pleased to tell you in detail, and usually with good humor. But don't ask just after a football (soccer) match, when local feelings run high and tribal warfare is close at hand.

Britain has long been a melting pot for other nations and cultures. Immigrants came originally from Europe, fleeing from wars or oppression. More recently they have come from the Commonwealth—a remnant of the empire that Britain established during 18th- and 19th-centuries, and forswore after World War II. Most recently of all they come from Asia, Africa, and eastern Europe, seeking a better life than they had back home. The stereotypical British male (pink-skinned, Protestant, with clipped-accent, bowler hat, pinstripe suit, and a job in the office) may never truly have existed. If he did, he has now gone for good. Modern Britons come in every possible skin tone, support any religious faith or none, speak any of a dozen languages, hold several different jobs before they are 30, and wear pretty-well what they choose in a hotchpotch of patterns and hues.

Natural Color

But back to the colors of Britain: where do we find them? First in nature, in the rocks and soils, the atmosphere, the plant cover. We occupy a spot where Earth's crust has been raised, lowered, thrown into folds, fragmented, and carved by glaciers and encroaching seas, providing a range of geological formations and colors. To some, the cliffs of Dover (see pages 84–85) are symbols of Albion (yet another ancient name for Britain). Inland, a broad band of sandstones, limestones, and shales

The lush rolling countryside of Kent (preceding pages) contrasts with the dramatic rock formations of the Roaches and Hen Cloud in the Peak District (above).

crosses the country obliquely from Bristol to the Tyne, yielding cliffs and crags in every hue from buff to iron-red. British landscape artists loved them—loved too the walls and vernacular buildings to which they gave rise. The honey-gold cottages of the Cotswolds and north Yorkshire, the gleaming spires of Oxford, and the burned-ocher crescents of Bath were all quarried close at hand. The Portland stone facing many London buildings was carried by sea from quarries in Dorset. Blue Welsh slates keep the rain off buildings far beyond the Welsh borders. Clays from different regions are baked into the millions of red, pink, dun, and yellow bricks that built most British houses and factories. Polished granites and marbles from all over the country bring color to shop-fronts, floors, kitchen counters, and graveyards.

Britain's dismal climate has much to answer for. The world's most extensive empire was founded, we are told, by Britons who could no longer stand the weather back home. But a damp maritime climate provides for a long growing season. In late winter, when the rest of Europe is blanketed in snow, Britain is already greening toward spring. For good measure, a damp atmosphere generates spectacular dawns and sunsets, again to the delight of Britain's landscape artists.

'Our England is a garden,' wrote the poet Rudyard Kipling, adding that '…such gardens are not made/By singing—'Oh, how beautiful!' and sitting in the shade…' He was right in one important sense. Britain's countryside, however natural-looking, is virtually all man-made. We have no true wilderness: almost everything that grows in gardens, fields, plantations, even moorlands, is a result of human management. Mercifully, it is predominantly a green garden, showing far more color and variety than the original forest provided.

Only fragments of native habitat remain, now carefully cherished and protected, but the farms, parklands, and woodlands that replace it show a creditable range of greens through spring and summer, and a matching set of browns, reds, and gold in fall. Nothing in Britain approaches the solid crimson of New England maples in the fall. But have you seen British moorlands in late summer, massed with purple heather? Or the glowing russets and reds of hedgerows, coppices, and orchards, with late apples and plums for the picking, and the leaves about to fall? Or a canary-yellow oil-seed rape field in the late spring? But we'll pass over that.

Of gardens themselves, Britain has an unmatched selection, from tiny domestic inner-city patches to the manicured acres of country mansions. Front gardens with lawn and privet (now often paved over for the family car), back gardens with washing line, potting-shed, and flowers; cottage gardens, herb gardens, rose gardens, walled gardens; gardens formal and regimented, gardens informal, casual and tatty; allotments (small portions of land rented out for cultivation) with prize celery and leeks—all pay tribute to a compelling British eccentricity. People need to grow things, in particular things that bring color, flavor, and a sense of achievement to mundane everyday life.

A Colorful Country

Birds, reptiles, and insects employ patches of vivid color as signals in threat, courtship, and other significant interactions. Humans have no such natural signals: it is perhaps no real loss, but we lack even the brightly hued faces of some of our close monkey kin. To compensate, in every human culture we borrow or steal color to decorate ourselves, our homes, our territories, our possessions.

Bicycling and walking are popular activities especially in the many national parks and along a network of footpaths. The quiet roads of the Lake District (above) allow peaceful bicycling.

First we used vegetable dyes, pigments from colored clays, and other natural products. As demand increased, whole industries arose to provide a wide range of colors applicable in every walk of life.

The British people are very good at color. British men, like men the world over, claim that women are the self-decorating gender. But tell that to a Royal Marine colonel in full dress uniform, to scarlet-coated guards at Buckingham Palace, to peers at the opening of Parliament, to mauve-

gowned judges, bishops in their Sunday best, to academics in velvet hats and crimson gowns, to Highlanders in bright tartans. They'll tell you that it's all very traditional, essential to the well-being of state and society, and the world will fall apart if they desist. You don't have to believe them. These costumes were invented, or at least restyled, in Victorian times, when everyone but Gilbert and Sullivan (composer and author of operettas) took such things seriously.

For color to be used so universally is a relatively new development. In medieval Britain, expensive colored fabrics were reserved for the ruling classes, while commoners wore drab hues. Colored paintings and tiles decorated churches, palaces, and mansions, but not farmsteads or cottages. In the 17th century, at the time of the Civil War, Puritans declared all decoration the devil's work: color was outlawed and respectable folk wore black. Restoration of the monarchy brought a return of color, in

particular to clothing and household fabrics, as a symbol of wealth and well-being. Regency and early Victorian eras were colorful for the prosperous, though still penny-plain for the rapidly expanding proletariat. The industrial production of cheap dyes from coal in the mid-19th century brought about a minor revolution, allowing almost everyone a splash of inexpensive color in a hatband, a scarf, or a necktie.

It took a further century and a much greater revolution to produce the riot of multi-hued plastics and fabrics we see around us today. Few under the age of 60 will recall the drabness of daily life in post-World War II Britain, when smoke made grit and grime universal, and walls, clothes, and furnishing fabrics were uniformly dun-colored to avoid showing the dirt. Along with the plastics and new fabrics came detergents, powerful alternatives to soap, which washed whiter, enhanced colors, and made cleaning easier. So did the new generation of cheap and efficient washing machines and vacuum cleaners. Cheap power tools and the do-it-yourself movement made everyone a decorator, helped by inexpensive magazines that, for better or worse, set new fashions and told everyone how to improve their homes, gardens, and environment.

This book, then, shows Britain as it is—a lively island with colorful landscapes, gardens, food, cities and towns, people and customs. Arrive on an overcast winter's day, and you might be disappointed: Britain and its people may look gray and dull. But be patient. Of the weather Britons say grandly 'If you don't like it, just wait an hour or two and it will change.' If it is as bad as that, it can only change for the better. Find a bright, cozy pub, enjoy a meal and a drink, and as if by magic, a more colorful Britain will appear.

Britain's coast is dotted with small fishing ports and harbours such as the one at Boscastle in Cornwall (right). Many settlements developed that depended on fishing but now they are often equally popular with summertime visitors.

Britain is unlikely to top your listing of countries renowned for good food. Unless, that is, you've visited recently and dropped in for lunch at a decent country pub. If you're new to the game, choose one from the *AA Pub Guide*: it may add a bit to the bill, but it shortens the odds of finding a good place considerably. Follow your nose toward the kitchen window: there should be an appetizing smell of good food, well cooked.

Britain is renowned for seafood, and why not? As a politician once pointed out, Britain is '…made mainly of coal and surrounded by fish.' Coal fueled the Industrial Revolution: local fish gave the country cheap, wholesome food and the fishing industry trained men to the sea, making Britain a maritime nation. But it is a nation of farmers too, producing acres of year-round vegetables, not to mention good-quality beef, lamb, pork, bacon, poultry, and game.

There is not much left of Britain's deep-sea fishing industry, but at any of a hundred small seaports along the coast you'll still find inshore fishermen at work. Their boats are high-tech, their methods age-old. Making and managing lobster pots (right), baiting long lines for haddock and halibut, and knowing where and when to catch crab, cod, herring, and mackerel in season—these are still the essentials of a highly skilled trade. And there's often a handy quayside café or outdoor restaurant ready to serve up the catch fresh from the sea (see pages 22–23).

22

MARKETS

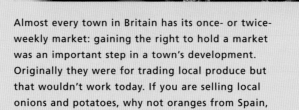

Almost every town in Britain has its once- or twice-weekly market: gaining the right to hold a market was an important step in a town's development. Originally they were for trading local produce but that wouldn't work today. If you are selling local onions and potatoes, why not oranges from Spain, tomatoes from the Netherlands and mushrooms from halfway across the country as well? Not to mention pineapples, grapefruit, melons, and year-round apples from the other side of the world.

Markets are attractive showcases for local produce. This spring display of daffodils and vegetables (top) is in Leyburn, North Yorkshire. Open-air stallholders set up shop at first light and take down their stalls in the evening. That is hard work, especially in winter, and bad weather can ruin a day's trading. The alternative is an enclosed arcade (above left), more expensive to rent, but more comfortable for sellers and buyers alike. Still, outdoor markets have their appeal, like this particularly colorful one in Norwich (above right).

THE LINEN BASKET

APPLES

Apples grow best in a temperate climate, with hard winters to kill off pests, warm springs to encourage the flowers and pollinating insects, and summer rain to fill out the fruit. Sunny slopes in southern Britain and the west country prove almost ideal: most of the country's orchards are found there.

More than 1,000 years of cultivation has produced hundreds of varieties; early-season apples for immediate eating, later ones for cooking and keeping, and small, sour varieties for cider-making. Apple pies, apple charlotte, apple crumble—there are dozens of local recipes for cooking apples. You like apple pie with ice-cream? Try it with a slice of Yorkshire cheese. Britain doesn't grow enough apples to last the year, so in winter, those in the shops may have been grown in Australia or New Zealand. They're good, but not half as good as a fresh home-grown apple straight from the tree.

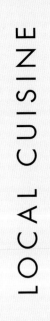

LOCAL CUISINE

We have a lot of local dishes (from far left to above right), best sampled close to their point of origin. Fish and chips? The fish needs to be fresh, doused in batter, deep-fried in beef dripping, and served with salt and vinegar, preferably on a sheet of newsprint to absorb some of the grease. English breakfast? Bacon, egg, sausage, mushrooms, tomato; to keep you going all day. Roast beef and Yorkshire pudding? Serve with roast potatoes, fresh vegetables, piquant horseradish sauce and gravy. Cornish tea? Scones, clotted cream, jam (jelly) and a pot of tea. Ploughman's lunch? It used to be fresh bread, cheese and pickles, and a pint of ale, but modern upscale ploughmen demand butter, lettuce, and tomatoes too. Malt whisky and oatmeal biscuits? Scots may tell you a good dram is a meal in itself: non-Scots prefer to eat something with it, to keep them from getting overexcited.

GROWING

Britons live constantly at odds with their climate—it is usually too hot or too cold, too wet or too dry, too windy, foggy, stormy, damp, or sunless. The country lies under a patch of atmosphere where rival air masses compete constantly for space. You'd think by now they'd be used to their

wrangling and jockeying for position. At least the weather provides a standard topic for conversation with strangers. At best, it adds up to a splendid climate for growing things, providing a succession of crops of delicious fruit and vegetables from late spring onward. Soft fruits do particularly well.

These strawberries, cherries, and raspberries (above) could be the makings of a simple, delicate summer pudding.

Britain grows a remarkable range of cereals, herbs, vegetables, oil-seeds, flowers, and other useful crops, shifting emphasis with changing markets, farm subsidies, and climate. Massive acreages produce wheat, barley, oats, hay and other cattle fodder, and grass for sheep and dairy herds. Bulbs are grown in Lincolnshire, lavender in Norfolk, sugar beet in Cambridgeshire, rhubarb in Yorkshire, and cabbages, sprouts, carrots, celery, and other kitchen crops wherever soils, climate, and markets permit. Oil-seed rape (following pages), adds vivid yellow to the late-spring landscape.

TRADITION

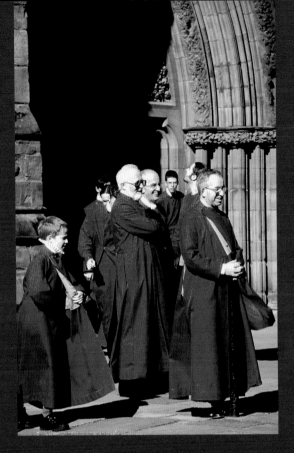

No visitor goes far in Britain without running into some piece of mild lunacy or eccentricity—like this otherwise harmless-looking gentleman (far left), wearing knee-breeches and triangular hat, who disturbs the peace by shouting loudly and ringing a handbell. 'It's tradition,' say those in the know, as though that explains everything.

He is a town crier: his functions are now vested, more effectively though with less élan, in TV newsreaders. He is not alone: tradition determines the dress and deportment of all the other colorful folk on these pages, and penetrates deeply into almost every aspect of British life. A good thing or bad? Probably a bit of both. The Brits would feel poorer without traditions, but they lose some and create new ones every day.

Red-cassocked choristers (top) enjoy a break from singing outside Carlisle Cathedral.
Oxford University dons (above) parade to the Sheldonian Theatre for a degree-awarding ceremony.

Military veterans, wearing World War II medals, take in the sunshine at Chelsea Royal Hospital, London (above). The hospital, founded by King Charles II in 1682, and designed and built by Sir Christopher Wren, provided originally for elderly or disabled soldiers who had served in the recent Civil and Dutch wars. Maintained as a charity, it is currently home to some 350 'Chelsea pensioners,' who wear a distinctive uniform of tricorn hat and long coat (red in summer, blue in winter), based on 17th-century military dress. Visitors are welcome to meet and talk to the pensioners, and visit their gardens, museum, chapel, and souvenir shop. Come on May 29 (Oak-apple Day), when the pensioners parade to honor their founder.

Most Britons in the early 19th century were still bound to farming and rural crafts. Two centuries later, in an industrial or indeed post-industrial society, they hanker for a simple, healthy rural life. Simple it may have been, but healthy it was not: many country folk quickly exchanged grinding rural poverty for marginally less grinding labor in the growing towns and cities. But we still honor the skills of earlier generations, and the modern craftsmen and women who take the trouble to learn and practise them. Here (left) a basket-maker weaves withies, a potter fashions clay into pots, and a mason builds a dry-stone wall. A glass-blower (above left) measures a delicate flask, and a woodturner (above right) crafts a lamp standard from timber, using ancient techniques with a modern twist. Electricity powers the furnace and lathe, but the skills are as old as the hills.

The woman above is spinning: her treadle-wheel is modern, though based on a traditional design. It is a gentle, soothing craft, not for those in a hurry. The treadle rocks, the wheel hums, the spun thread lengthens and is gathered into a skein for weaving or knitting. Fingers and thumbs are softened by the wool's natural oils.

A thatcher (above right)—a modern practitioner of an old, old craft—lays straw or reeds on the roof to keep the rain out. Why not tiles or slates? Because there are many areas of Britain where they would have had to be brought in from miles away. Thatch is warmer in winter and cooler in summer, and lasts just as long—a straw roof for 20 years, a reed roof four or five times longer.

Of all animals that have contributed to Britain's prosperity, the British owe the most to the humble sheep. Ancient Britons stole their skins and wore them entire, but then word got around that wool was a renewable resource, one that could be sheared (above), carded, dyed, spun, skeined, and knitted or woven into more versatile fabrics. Here a shearer starts the process, stripping a fleece with electric shears.

A century ago the blacksmith (above) was a key figure in village and town: every horse went to work on two pairs of shoes that the blacksmith heated and hammered to fit. Today he's more likely to be making decorative ironware—gates and railings, perhaps—but his craft still demands fire and anvil, hammer and tongs, and a lot of skill and muscle to bring it all together.

They've been making pots in Britain for well over 3,000 years. Fragments frequently turn up in spadefuls of earth, often with a story to tell through shape, texture, or decoration. In the busy 21st century, when goods are mass-produced and sold by the million, there are still artisans who craft pots from clay, purely for the joy of it (above left).

With so much beautiful scenery up and down the country, it's not surprising that Britain has a tradition of landscape painters (above right). Not only Turner and Constable—dozens of lesser masters and hundreds of gifted amateurs have been inspired to have a go. Tearooms and coffee bars are often full of their paintings: you can admire them free or pick up a very acceptable memento for a few pounds.

ARTISTS

Color-printed books and magazines in every home, eye-catching advertisements on every hoarding, vivid posters on every wall—they are all offspring of the color revolution that hit post-war Britain in the 1950s. However loud and dazzling, however quiet and tasteful, they are often the produce of

artists, designers, and craftsmen and women who work in small print studios up and down the country (above left).

Original English silverware is much in demand for its elegance, traditional design, and sturdy lasting value. There is modern silverware too, also much

sought-after today and likely to retain its value well into the future. This silversmith (above), heir to a long tradition, combines art and age-old skills, repairing and renovating the old, as well as creating the new.

FOLK TRADITIONS

Not everyone in Britain wears a botanical hat. To qualify, you need to join a traditional dance troupe, be willing to wear bells and flowers and dance in public places to squeeze-boxes, pipes, and drums. That takes energy, time, and devotion but continues traditions that go back hundreds of years.

In Grasmere, in Cumberland in the Lake District, there still exists a traditional form of wrestling (top). It looks gentle, even conciliatory, but this is just the start. The contestants are sizing each other up: in a moment one or other will be on the ground. Those dazzling briefs, worn (like Superman's) outside the long-johns, are a modern concession.

Head farther north and you're into Scotland, where dancing tends toward the well-dressed and balletic. If, toward the end of a party, you have ever bungled your way through an eightsome reel or a set of Gay Gordons, you'll appreciate the skill and grace of a Scottish dance done properly, by people who are dressed for the occasion, and know beyond doubt what to do next (above).

SPORT
& LEISURE

Epsom in Surrey is known for its racecourse (top),
which draws crowds especially in June when the
Oaks and the Derby are run. Cricket, played in its
simplest form on a village green is an enduring
summer sight (above), as is golf, which was
introduced to England in around 1608.

Sails were traditionally made from white, gray, or red-brown canvas, while hot-air balloons and airships were of fine silver-painted cotton or linen. Today they're both made from woven plastic fabrics, in any shade that is bright and cheerful enough to attract attention.

You can see much of Britain through a train window or car windscreen. As a walker, you see, smell, and feel it too, in the quiet, sublime corners where neither roads nor railways penetrate. These long-distance walkers are enjoying the view across Buttermere in the Lake District.

Two seamen, a writer, and a queen—just four of the thousands of statues that commemorate celebrities from the past. On Plymouth Hoe, 16th-century privateer and admiral Sir Francis Drake (above) stares seaward for his first sighting of the Spanish Armada. Rumor has it that he was playing bowls when the Spanish fleet hove into sight, and he finished his game before he dealt with them. Robert Burns (above right), Scottish writer and social renegade, ponders his next poem in the high street of his hometown, Dumfries. No other British poet has appealed so profoundly to so wide an audience, not only in Britain but across the world. They celebrate Burns Night in Scotland, but on New Year's Eve they sing Auld Lang Syne even in China. Outside Buckingham Palace, in the heart of her capital, Queen-Empress Victoria (right) stares glumly at the London traffic. In her day you

traveled horse-drawn or by 'Shanks's pony' (an obscure British expression for walking). Today it's all petrol and diesel, and London's air is filled with traffic fumes.

Admiral and Viscount Horatio Nelson (far right), most beloved of British sea dogs, takes a lofty view from his column in Trafalgar Square in the capital. Raised a quarter of a century after his death in 1805, his memorial is perhaps London's most celebrated landmark, and a popular pigeon roost.

STATUES

Blenheim Palace in Oxfordshire, was built between 1705 and 1722 by the first Duke of Marlborough—a gift from the nation for his victories in war. Named for his most celebrated battle, and designed by Sir John Vanbrugh, it stands in an estate laid out by renowned landscape architect 'Capability' Brown.

To some, Blenheim is the world's most perfect baroque palace. To others it is a tasteless yell of triumph, a monstrous pile ruining an Oxfordshire valley. Neither John Churchill, the First Duke, nor Sarah his wife, lived to enjoy it as we see it today. By the time Blenheim was finished, he was senile, she driven to distraction by the problems of putting it together. But Blenheim is well worth a visit. Less than half an hour by road from Oxford, the setting is indeed delightful, the furnishings and fittings tell us much about 18th-century taste, and Woodstock pubs do very good lunches.

CASTLES & PALACES

Norman warlords and their successors built castles to hold their land and protect families and followers. Lesser landowners built fortified houses as late as the 16th century and added token fortifications even later. By the early 18th century, when there was no longer need for cannon-proof walls and turret windows, wealthy folk built palaces instead. Architects produced elegant designs with classical overtones. Landscape gardeners created lakes and vistas, and the fortunate owners filled their palaces with statues, friezes, urns, paintings, and other artifacts bought or 'acquired' on tours of Europe.

Historic buildings up and down the land remind us of times when power lay in the hands of the elite. Castles especially were places of fear, to be entered by the common man only at his peril. Today, most of Britain's historic buildings are maintained by the National Trust or English Heritage, and a few by hereditary owners, who defray expenses by opening to the public. The common man buys his ticket at the door, with some certainty of coming out alive at closing time.

BLACK & WHITE

While the wealthy, bidden by fashionable architects, imported stone from afar for their houses, simpler folk made do with what lay to hand. Often this was oak from the local forest, combined with rubble or soft stone faced with lime plaster—creating the black-and-white buildings that can still be found all over Britain. Originally they were gray and white, like the simple countryman's house (left). Solid, well-seasoned oak ages to silver-gray (see p.61) and does not need painting: the 'white' between the beams is lime-wash, made cream-colored and weatherproof with animal fat. Black tarry paints, applied to protect inferior timber, with stark white plaster, became the vogue in Victorian times. Black-and-white building is seen at its best in this Chester town house (above).

Pointed Gothic arches and multi-ribbed stone buttresses (top left) frame the windows of Peterborough Cathedral in Cambridgeshire. An echo of Georgian elegance in the simple front doors of Port Sunlight (above), an early 20th-century housing scheme on the Wirral Peninsula.

Dormer windows (top center), capped with Cotswold slates, light the roof space in these south Gloucestershire cottages in Arlington Row, Bibury. The Norman arches of Jedburgh Abbey (above), just north of the English-Scottish border. Built in 1118, the abbey was ruined in border warfare in 1523.

An architect's fancy: an elaborately decorated stone eye sits in the wall of Norwich Cathedral in Norfolk (top). Severely functional: a no-nonsense 19th-century sash window, set in a pastel–tinted house wall, in Culross in Scotland (above).

DOORS, WINDOWS, & ARCHWAYS

A window (top) bearing the royal monogram GRI in art nouveau style, in the royal waiting room of Ballater Station, Deeside, Scotland. Elegant windows (above) in a clean-cut Georgian façade in Glenfinlas Street, in Edinburgh's New Town, built in the late 18th and early 19th

centuries. A delicate wrought-iron mesh blends with tendrils of Virginia creeper (top) to protect a Gothic-style window of Christ Church, Oxford. Originally a firing point (above), but now filled in and glazed to make a small but serviceable window in Claypotts Castle in Dundee, Scotland.

Leaded windows (top) in the timber-framed Little Hall in Lavenham, Suffolk, a medieval town that prospered due to a flourishing wool trade. Colonnaded windows (above) form the frontage of a row of 18th-century houses in the Circus in Bath, near the Somerset–Gloucestershire border.

MODERNIST

Like a huge, slowly-turning bicycle wheel, with self-rotating gondolas, the London Eye (left) dominates the south bank of the Thames, providing staggering pigeons'–eye views of the capital city. The Luna Light Building (above), a stylish former factory in Glasgow in Scotland.

The transparent domes (top left) of the Eden Project (open to visitors all year) nestle in an old quarry near St. Austell in Cornwall. The domes house tropical and warm-temperate plants in controlled environments. The gardens illustrate plants used for foods, medicines, and fabrics.

They've been busy in the Harbourside area of Bristol, converting an old Great Western Railway shed into a new educational building called Explore (top right). The huge ball, 50ft (15m) in diameter and covered with stainless steel panels, is a planetarium.

Over 30 miles (48km) from Trafalgar Square, deep in the Essex countryside, Stansted (above) is the newest and the farthest-flung of London's airports. If you are in a hurry, a fast rail link gets you to town quickly. If you are not, take a little time to appreciate the structure of this modern terminal.

The railroads that crept across Britain from the mid-19th century onward were built with flair and imagination. Architects who designed the main London terminals—Isambard Brunel at Paddington in 1850, W. H. Barlow at St. Pancras in 1868—created strong, cathedral-like buildings, combining new iron-girder-and-glass technology with traditional styles of decoration. However, the stations soon lost their gloss as the coal-fueled locomotives belched smoke that obliterated color and fine detail. With the advent of diesel and electric power, new techniques for cleaning,

and an appreciation of Victorian enterprise, the quality of the buildings is being revealed. These pages show archways at St. Pancras Station (left), Oriel windows in Paddington Station (top), Paddington station roof (right) and the iron girders of the roof of St. Pancras station (above).

TIMBER & STONE

The bigger the building, the bigger the problem of spanning the roof. Early builders solved it with simple cylindrical pillars and arches, here seen in the nave of Tewkesbury Abbey (above) built in the early 12th century. Rounded Romanesque or Norman arches link the pillars, and still-rounded but more complex cross-arching or vaulting supports the roof.

By the mid-16th century, when Henry VIII commissioned King's College Chapel, Cambridge (right), builders had learned to build taller and wider. Fluted pillars, supported outside by buttresses, soared and divided into complex fan vaulting, creating an enormous, resonant, and well-lit space within.

Timber buildings, like this splendid 14th-century tithe barn at Bredon in Worcestershire (top), and the market cross at Somerton in Somerset (above), solved the same problems with elaborations of solid wooden buttresses and cross beams, each placed with geometrical precision to spread the load evenly.

Pubs ('public houses') began as 'inns'; places to stopover with shelter and sustenance for wayfarers, selling home-brewed ale (safer than water), simple food, and with stabling for horses. Over the years they have come a long way: now they are perhaps Britain's most cherished institutions. They still sell drinks and food (often some of the best in town), and many have overnight accommodation. Stabling has gone, but there is usually a parking lot. Local differences in licensing laws have led to subtle differences between English, Welsh, and Scottish pubs. This wine bar in Leith, the port of Edinburgh (left), for example, looks more like a shop than a British pub (above), though you won't know for sure until you get inside. Then a typical city pub (top right) can provide a completely different atmosphere from a country pub with a garden (right). Try them all, or as many as you can.

PUBS

GREEN LAND, BLUE SEA

Britain's damp, maritime climate makes it a predominantly green country—not emerald-green like neighboring Ireland (which is even damper), but nonetheless recognizable as the 'green and pleasant land' of William Blake's poem. Much of it is flat or gently undulating: there are modest mountains in the north and west, but alpine ranges, if they ever existed, were long ago ground to stumps by glaciation. In this small island, with its sinuous coastline, few places lie more than 75 miles (125km) from the sea. Almost every wind, from whichever direction, begins or ends as a sea breeze.

So Britain offers a splendid selection of land- and seascapes—scenes that change dramatically within just a few miles. Never take a book on a train journey: there's so much to see through the window.

Legend has it that Britain is a built-up area, but don't believe a word of it. Well over 90 percent is still field, forest, or moorland, providing a patchwork of vivid shades and textures that shift harmoniously with the seasons. Most of Britain's native trees are deciduous, changing color as the leaves grow, mature, and fall. Much of the land remains forested, and trees grow freely along field boundaries, helping to shelter livestock in winter. Acres of rich pasture provide summer forage for sheep and cattle, and meadows yellow-green with buttercups yield hay for winter feed.

It's a patchwork pattern, in which the patches tend to grow bigger. In upland areas the small fields are separated by stone walls (above), a pattern right for grazing. In the lowlands, walls, fences, and hedges are disappearing as farmers need space to operate bigger, more cost-effective machinery.

In the far southwest corner of Britain rises a dome of hard, silvery granite, capped by moorland and rough grazing. This is Dartmoor (above), made famous by Victorian novelists, and the site of an older but still-operational jail. Dartmoor has a general elevation of about 1,000ft (300m), rising to just over 2,000ft (600m) in the northwest corner. Ancient hill forts tell of pre-Roman occupation: scattered spoil tips, now long abandoned, represent centuries of mining for lead, tin, and other ores. Now much of Dartmoor is a national park attracting summer walkers and rock climbers.

Northern England has a different kind of moorland (right)—slopes of wild grassland, bracken, and heath rise steeply from fertile valleys. Northerners call them 'fells,' and the hardy enjoy fell-walking, which leads them along wild but well-trodden upland tracks.

Northwestern England, just short of the Scottish border, is dominated by uplands of hard volcanic rock, ringed centrifugally by deep glacier-carved valleys, and jeweled by long, narrow lakes. This is the Lake District (or just 'The Lakes'), and it is England's most mountainous, most scenic, most popular, and wettest area. Keswick (above), a market town on Derwentwater, is one of the smaller lakes. Its sturdy lakeside mansions, and others like them, provide hospitality for thousands of summer visitors. Behind rises Skiddaw (3,054ft/931m), basking in late fall sunshine, with a dusting of snow that warns of winter to come. The Lakes are lovely, but chances are you'll need an umbrella.

Britain measures over 630 miles (1,000km) from Land's End to John o'Groats in the Scottish Highlands, and 300 miles (480km) across its midriff. But it is not difficult to calculate that there is at least 3,000 miles (4,800km) of coastline, possibly twice as much if you figure in all the deeply indented bays, bights, estuaries, and islands. Not surprisingly, this tally includes all possible kinds of coasts, from low, sandy beaches (top right and above) to towering cliffs.

Before roads, canals, and railways crisscrossed the land, coastal waters, estuaries, and rivers were the main highways. Coastal seamen played the role of today's truck, van, and bus drivers, most of them in ships far smaller than this three-master (top left).

WATER'S EDGE

A derelict ship is a sad sight, doubly so when its reason for being has also disappeared. On a cobbled strand on the island of Mull, off the west coast of Scotland, a small cargo ship and smaller fishing boat (above) rot quietly together. The cargo ship was a coaster, successor to dozens of coal-fired 'puffers' that once plied the sounds and channels of western Scotland, bringing goods and news to tiny coastal settlements. When the roads came, coasters disappeared, replaced by trucks and vans. Small fishing boats served for a time, then became obsolete, to be replaced by others that were larger, faster, easier to maintain, or cheaper to run. With paint fading, ironwork rusting and timbers shrinking, these two have earned an honorable retirement.

EROSION

Britain is eroding and in some places quickly enough to be noticeable. Along the east coast, towns and villages have disappeared since medieval times. The culprit is the sea, rolling around the coast, adding a bit here, taking away there, and overall gobbling up the land. The sea-level is rising but Britain is tilting too, upward in the north and down in the south.

On this remote beach in northern Scotland (left) the sea has created a tasteful array of colored pebbles, planting a driftwood tree stump for good measure. It has isolated a headland in Dorset, southern England, carving an arch (above left) that it will ultimately destroy. The Needles (above) are off the western end of the Isle of Wight. Once a continuous limestone headland, erosion has reduced them to a row of battered teeth.

Following pages: Seven Sisters on the south coast.

STILL STANDING

Stonehenge (top), not far from Salisbury in southern England, was built over a period of 2,000 years, ending 3,500 years ago. The objectives of the builders changed over time, but must have been remarkably important, as massive 4-ton stones were hauled in from south Wales, 240 miles (380km) away. The Castlerigg stone circle (above right) is a smaller and much simpler henge, probably of similar age, one of hundreds dotting the countryside all over Britain. Again, many people went to a lot of trouble to set them up. Hadrian's Wall (top right) was nobody's idea of fun. Extending from the Firth of Solway, close to Carlisle, to the mouth of the Tyne, it was built in the time of the Roman emperor Hadrian to mark the northern limit of the empire, and keep out marauding northern tribesmen. Who built it? The British working man, under duress, and very

hard work it must have been. Were they temples? Celestial calendars? Memorials? We do not know. The Long Man of Wilmington (above left) is less of a puzzle. Measuring 226ft (69m) from top to toe, he was carved in the turf of a chalk downland by unknown locals in the 18th century, a crude copy of much older figures of men and horses that appear elsewhere along the downs. So far as we know, he was just for fun.

CULTURE
& STYLE

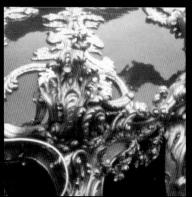

BRITISH ICONS

Britain has never been short of artists, nor lacking in culture or style. For centuries imperial Britain conferred British values on its colonies but those days are gone. Modern British art, culture, and style are more for domestic use, for the comfort and enjoyment of the British people. There is quiet satisfaction from the complex Union Flag, monstrous telephone and mail boxes, and the simple clarity of the London Underground logo. The Brits relish the lunacy of London's Lord Mayor's show and wouldn't wish it on anyone else. Englishmen envy Scots their tartans and flock to the Edinburgh Festival, and everyone enjoys the summer funfair. The seaside, with its range of icons, is only a bus ride away, and there's theater, opera, and art for everyone in modern Britain.

The Union Flag combines the crosses of the patron saints of England, Scotland, and Ireland. The cross of St. George (red on a white background) overlies those of St. Andrew (diagonal white on a blue background) and St. Patrick (diagonal red on white), the latter slightly offset.

Traditional telephone boxes in red-painted cast iron and glass, have stood for generations, foursquare and dependable, on city streets, village greens, windswept moors, and storm-lashed pier-heads. With the advent of mobile phones they are being phased out.

London acquired its first part-underground railway line, the Metropolitan, in 1863. Now a dozen lines combine to form the London Underground Railway, crisscrossing the capital and serving a ring of suburbs. Used every day by millions, its stations are marked by these simple roundels (above).

A guardsman in dress uniform on sentry duty at Windsor Castle (above), guards his Queen. The leek collar flashes and the ten buttons down the tunic, arranged five and five, tell us that he is a Welsh Guard. He may look like a toy, but don't be misled: he's a trained soldier from a disciplined regiment.

The London street sign (above right) tells us that Oxford Street is part of the City of Westminster, and for letter and parcel delivery, in the smart West 1 postal district. The dual language on the Brick Lane sign (top), in the East 1 district, tells us that this area has a large Asian community.

Britain takes its mail boxes seriously: typically they are 'pillar boxes'—cast-iron cylinders set into the ground, painted red, and bearing the royal crest. They are usually single, but the one in the grounds of Windsor Castle is for the Queen's letters.

PAGEANTRY

In general, Britons are not demonstrative, but the crowds always turn out for a royal wedding, state funeral, or the annual Lord Mayor's Show. Out come the uniforms and decorations and the gilded horse-drawn coaches that emerge from hiding on the day of the parade, then disappear until the next one. Not so the soldiers—the Horse Guards and Welsh Guards bandsmen—for whom parading is a part of the job.

The splendid horse-drawn coach (far left) is the Lord Mayor of London's coach, parading through the City. Come rain or sunshine, the show happens on the second Saturday in November every year. Ringed by a bodyguard from the Company of Pikemen and Musketeers, the newly elected Lord Mayor drives through the City to the Royal Courts of Justice, where he takes the oath of office. For him it is the start of a very busy year.

Scots have a pageantry all of their own, based on deep loyalties to land, kin, and traditions. Hence the kilts, the sporrans (decorated purses), the bagpipes and the tartans, and the determination to show that they come from north of the English-Scottish border. Traditional Highland dress was *plaid*, a length of woven woolen fabric, usually self-colored or checkered, wrapped around the waist to form a kilt, with the end thrown over the shoulder. Weaving-in crisscross patterns of colored stripes to create distinctive tartans, and linking the tartans to clans or families, are relatively modern developments. But tartan remains a distinctly Scottish design, which certainly makes for a brighter Scotland.

TARTAN

Many Scots emigrated during the 18th and 19th centuries, settling mainly in Canada, the United States, Australia, and New Zealand. Their descendants gather to keep alive Scottish traditions of dress, music, and dancing, like this pipe major at an international festival.

FUNFAIRS

Fairs began as gatherings for buying and selling on the very rare occasions of public holidays. They attracted crowds, and the crowds drew entertainers —conjurors, dancers, and musicians—who brought color and excitement. Today's equivalent is the funfair, perhaps an annual event like Hull Fair or Nottingham Goose Fair, or a permanent fixture in a seaside resort like Yarmouth or Southend.

At a funfair you no longer buy or sell sheep. You just have fun, riding the merry-go-rounds, sampling the sideshows, scaring yourself on the roller coaster, and jarring your teeth in the bumper cars.

THEATER

The stage in Britain reached its highest point in the late 19th and early 20th centuries, when every town and city had at least one theater for live performances. First the cinema, then radio and television, darkened and closed many venues. There's good reason for valuing those that are left.

The King's Theatre in Glasgow (left) enjoys a nearly full house, from stalls to boxes and gallery. So does the Globe (top), a replica of Shakespeare's theater on the South Bank in London. The open-air Minack Theatre (above) replicates a classical Greek theater, in the setting of a Cornish clifftop.

CULTURAL DIVERSITY

Britons find culture and enjoyment in many forms and situations, some unexpected. The small Cornish fishing-town of St. Ives finds room both for a museum devoted to sculptor Barbara Hepworth (left), and a branch of the prestigious Tate Gallery (top). Secondhand bookshops survive in almost every small town. 'The Angel of the North,' a winged statue more than 65ft (20m) high, dominates a hilltop above the Tyne Valley.

Hats rather than horses steal the show at a fashionable race meeting and opera-goers enjoy an open-air picnic at Glyndeborne in East Sussex (above right). Boating enthusiasts enjoy similar fare on the banks of the River Thames at the well-known rowing town of Henley-on-Thames (right).

Some regard the British Isles as uniformly, uncompromisingly damp. It is true that it's first to catch rain, sleet, or snow from the depressions that move in from the Atlantic and parade across Europe from west to east. Ireland gets it first: any inclement weather that hasn't already broken there, lands along the western seaboard of Britain from Cornwall to the Shetland Islands.

Among the wettest areas is the Lake District (well, where else would lakes come from?) with rainfall above 60in (150cm) per year. Parts of eastern Britain by contrast are semi-desert, with rainfall below 20in (50cm) per year.

Not many of us like rain, snow, or sleet while it is falling, but the streams, rivers, and standing water that result are very much part of the British scene. So are the cloudscapes, the mists (British poets grow very lyrical over these), the thin drizzle that so often obscures the horizon, and the clean, gorgeous light that blazes through once the rain has gone.

Rainbows appear when sunlight filters through rain. Folklore holds that there's a pot of gold at the end of every one. These rainbows have formed over Aberaeron, Dyfed, on the coast of Wales (top), and close to the town of Hawkshead, in the Lake District (above).

Not quite the highest peak in the Lake District, Scafell Pike (above) rises to 3,210ft (979m). Like many of its fellows, for much of the summer the peak is part-hidden by a shifting blanket of clouds about its shoulders. Early mornings are the best time for sightseeing in the Lakes, but you mustn't feel cheated if you don't see everything at once. Take time—allow a few days—and be prepared to travel about. The weather is usually patchy and can clear locally in a moment.

The converse is equally true: don't let a spell of clear weather tempt you up into the hills without adequate clothing. Take windproofs, waterproofs, and a flask of hot chocolate for when the cloud comes down. Another part of the country known for its changeable weather is the Isle of Skye. The brooding Cuillin Hills on this Scottish island (following pages) are dramatic at any time of year.

Not every British castle runs to a moat, but Caerphilly in south Wales (above), and Broughton Castle near Banbury in Oxford (right), both have standing water as part of their defenses. Moats were picturesque, and no doubt practical in keeping enemies at a distance. Unfortunately they were smelly in summer, a breeding ground for midges and mosquitoes, and the castles were perpetually damp.

Caerphilly Castle, built during the 13th century, is renowned for its leaning tower (to the right of the picture). Oliver Cromwell's troops tried unsuccessfully to blow the tower up during the Civil Wars of the 1640s: perhaps it seemed a good idea at the time. Caerphilly town is now also famous for its excellent cheese.

REFLECTIONS

Broughton Castle (above) started out as an early 14th-century manor house. A century later, when the neighbors were giving trouble, the owner fortified it, adding battlements and a gatehouse. In the more peaceful early 1600s, the Fiennes family (which still owns it today) added a couple of stories and large windows that gave them views of their parkland. Though still called a castle, it has been a sumptuous but comfortable family home for hundreds of years.

Neither moated nor crenellated, nor a showcase for wealth, Bedford House near Tenbury Wells in Worcestershire (above), is a product of more tranquil times. It's an elegant Georgian country house, calmly reflecting all that is simplest and best in English domestic architecture.

NATURE'S MIRROR

The view across a mirror-like lake at Buttermere in the Lake District in winter sunshine (above). Calm, with clear skies and a dusting of snow: the sort of weather when the air temperature plummets at night and the lake starts to freeze over. Not seriously at first: just an inch or two of clear ice.

But two or three nights will make it thick enough for skating.

Most visitors see the Lake District in summer, when the weather may be wet but is seldom cold, but winters can be tough. A lot of the land is above the 500ft (150m) contour, and long spells with

snow on the ground, coupled with strong winds and drifting snow, make life grim for grazing cattle and sheep and for the farmers who tend them. Spring comes eventually (right) and though hard-packed snow covers the tops, the grass starts to grow, yielding lush, safe grazing.

Tewkesbury (left) stands on a slight rise close to the junction of two rivers, the Severn and the Avon. Both kept it busy as an inland port: its riverside houses and Norman abbey tower reflect an earlier prosperity. Tewkesbury still thrives today, as a small but prosperous market town.

WATERSIDE

Loch Carron (above left) is one of a dozen or more sea-lochs that penetrate deep into the west coast of Scotland. On its sheltered inner reaches stands the village of Lochcarron, backed by the steep slopes of Carn nan Iomairean. Here the village views its own reflection in the calm waters of the loch.

The coast of Devon is dotted with tiny harbors serving villages once famous for their fishing. Brixham, south of Torbay (top), is just such a place. The fishing boats are still there, though the chunky little Brixham trawlers that helped in the early days of trawling are long gone.

Loch Fyne, another sea-loch on the west coast of Scotland, was once renowned for its herrings. The local laird, the Duke of Argyll, built the model town of Inverary (above) between 1746 and 1780. A pleasing little market town, it is a center for walkers in western Argyll.

CANALS

Like its railways, Britain's canals were originally cut for the use and convenience of industry. Over two centuries and more there developed a network of canals that became the country's main thoroughfares for transporting heavy goods. From early Victorian times railways began to supplant them. Later road and rail transport made them almost completely redundant.

But not entirely. By the early 20th century all but a few of the major canals were in decline, or had already become derelict. Then came a revival. A few enthusiasts realized that, once cut, the shallow trough of a canal is a positive asset, relatively easy to maintain and use. Less fussy and demanding than railroads, they pass serenely through miles of unspoilt countryside.

Canals that happen to head in the right direction can still be used economically to carry heavy goods.

Those that don't can simply be enjoyed—which is now most of them are used today. Not everyone may learn to drive a locomotive, but almost anyone can quickly learn to manage a slow-chugging narrow-boat. Canal travel is a restful way to move through the countryside. You can't hurry: the speed limit is four miles per hour, which leaves plenty of scope for enjoying the scenery. You can move when you like, moor almost anywhere along the bank, and stay as long as you please. Many inns that catered to the barge trade still exist and are ready to provide good food. There are locks to be negotiated, linking stretches of canal at different levels, but that is easy and part of the fun. The Shropshire Union Canal (left) runs through the West Midlands linking Shrewsbury with Chester. The Brecon & Monmouthshire Canal (above) wanders through the heart of Brecon Beacons.

WATERFALLS

Waterfalls need a lot of water to keep going. Not surprisingly we find them mostly along the wetter, Atlantic side of Britain, in Wales, the Lake District, and western Scotland. Wealthy property-owners of the 18th and 19th centuries greatly admired cascading water. If an estate didn't have a reasonable waterfall, it was up to the landscape architect to provide one. You can see why they were so popular: there is nothing more soothing than sitting by a massive flow of water, listening as it chuckles and gurgles its way to the sea. Owning a real waterfall, or even living close by one, was a great asset. These waterfalls are at Bowood House in Wiltshire in the south of England (far left), Clackmannanshire in Scotland (top) and Hardraw Force in Yorkshire in the north of England (above). The Swallow Falls are near Betws-y-coed in Snowdonia National Park in North Wales (right).

Montrose (left) is a small, ancient town on the
east coast of Scotland, on a spur between a huge
tidal basin and the sea. It's early morning, the tide
is out, and the sun rising over the town gives it a
special magic.

We've seen it before in broad daylight (see page
88), but here Stonehenge glistens in the light of
early dawn (above).

SPRING & SUMMER

Britain's winters are mild these days. It can snow as late as May, but we don't expect settled snow after March. Spring usually appears in the south by early April, in the north a little later: there's a change—not so much in the weather, as in our feelings about it. There's warmth in the sun, warm breezes dry the ground, and the lawn needs mowing.

Snowdrops and crocuses come and go, bees buzz in willows and apple blossom, daffodils give way to tulips and bluebells carpet the beechwoods. By early May it is truly spring. Scientists tell us the climate is warming. If so, grandmotherly advice to '…cast not a clout till May is out' (meaning 'keep your vest on') may no longer apply.

Around late May and early June, hedges blossom, grass verges burgeon with flowers, the first roses appear, and suddenly it's summer.

Woodlands and gardens come to life in spring. In gardens the heralds are crocuses and daffodils, in woodlands native bluebells (above left), that grow, flower and die back before the trees are in full leaf. Irises (above right) come later, though plant breeders have extended their season.

Lavender was probably introduced to Britain by the
Romans. Bush lavenders are among the glories of
any summer garden, with a soothing natural scent.
Lavender grows too as a commercial crop. If you
are in Norfolk at the right time of year, pay a visit
to one of its lavender farms.

SUMMER DAYS

It's high summer, vacation time, and the weather is gorgeous; let's spend a day on the beach. This is Weymouth, on the Dorset coast, a popular resort with a sandy beach and safe bathing.

FALLING LEAVES

By September summer is fast disappearing, and deciduous woodland all over Britain is changing color. The sun stays low in the sky, shadows are long, falling leaves form an ever-thickening carpet, and nuts make a feast for squirrels and jays. After a hot summer, fall often comes early, welcomed for its cooler nights and fresh, sparkling mornings. In woodlands all over Britain the colors can be quite staggering—gentle golds, browns and tans of oak, chestnut, ash, birch, sycamore, and beech. Horse chestnuts (above) are still seized eagerly by today's sophisticated children, to play conkers. And of course the harvest. The hay is already baled up in black or more colorful plastic wrappings, and golden sheaves are a thing of the past. But wheat, barley, oats, sugar beet, forage beans, and corn are ripening in the fields, to be brought in, one way or another, before the coming rains get them.

WINTER

Britons who vow they would never miss an English spring are usually less enthusiastic about winters. It is not winter cold they dread, nor even winter snow: many will head off to European ski resorts, where there is plenty of both. British winters, between late November and early March, tend just to be dreary, with long spells of sunless days, overcast skies, sharp winds, and cold, very wet rain. Short-term shifts in climate give older folk clear memories of 'different' seasons, including much harsher winters than the present ones—winters when hard, biting cold stilled the rivers and froze the pipes, when snow lay thick on the ground for weeks, stopping trains and traffic and holding up vital supplies.

It is worth remembering that something of the kind happens almost every year in Britain's thinly populated upland regions. Only when it happens

in the lowlands does it become remarkable. And when it does, unlike the hardy people of mainland Europe and North America, Britons are never quite prepared for it. Snow ploughs? Snow tires? Wheel chains? Let's just hope it warms up next week—and it usually does.

Cefn Cyff ridge, Brecon Beacons National Park (far left top); The North Downs, Hampshire (far left bottom); upland sheep (center) in Cwm Dergen Valley, Wales; winter sunshine over ice-bound lakes (top); icicles cascading from tussock grass (left); the heart of the Yorkshire Dales (above).

FARMING YEAR

For generations farming was the backbone of the British economy: in the late 19th century it was still a major employer. Today it plays a much smaller part, but many Britons still think of themselves as country folk, hanker for the rural life, and love livestock—or at least the idea of livestock, in farming as it used to be. Most chickens in Britain today live constrained lives in batteries. These strangely marked hens of a rare breed (top) belong to the Parke Farm in Devon.

Highland cattle (top right), stockily built, with handlebar horns and long woolly coats, are well-suited to winter conditions in the Scottish uplands. Special breeds of semiwild ponies (above left) live in several areas of Britain. These are New Forest ponies, found in the New Forest area of southwest Hampshire. Pigs once roamed wild through all Britain's extensive forest, but this

Tamworth (above left) leads a more sheltered, though probably shorter, life in a farmer's care. When farming was Britain's major industry, sheep were the mainstay of farming. Capable of surviving all but the hardest winters, yielding wool, skins, and meat, they were animals to be taken seriously.

Breeders produce dozens of different regional strains, suited to different conditions up and down the land. These white-faced Herdwicks (top) survive well in the harsh conditions of the Lake District. Ducks and geese too have a long and honorable history as domestic animals. Often the province of

the farmer's wife, they were reared in spring, grazing in self-sustaining flocks on common land, rivers, and ponds. Quick-growing geese could be herded to market, while those that survived into fall found a ready sale at Christmas.

ON THE MOVE

A long, narrow mainland and a scattering of islands—travel and transportation have always been problems in holding Britain together. The bus has, for well over a century, been Britain's major people-carrier: single-decked, double-decked, modified with extra comforts into the coach for long-distance travel.

Sea-going ferries have always been needed to link the mainland to the various islands. Catamarans (top left) cross to the Isle of Wight, while more conventional ferries link Ullapool in mainland Scotland, with Stornaway in the Hebrides.

Railways have served Britain for over 150 years, for both short- and long-distance travel. While streamlined modern trains streak importantly up and down the country, the British retain a special affection for local services, such as those that have been rescued from closure (above).

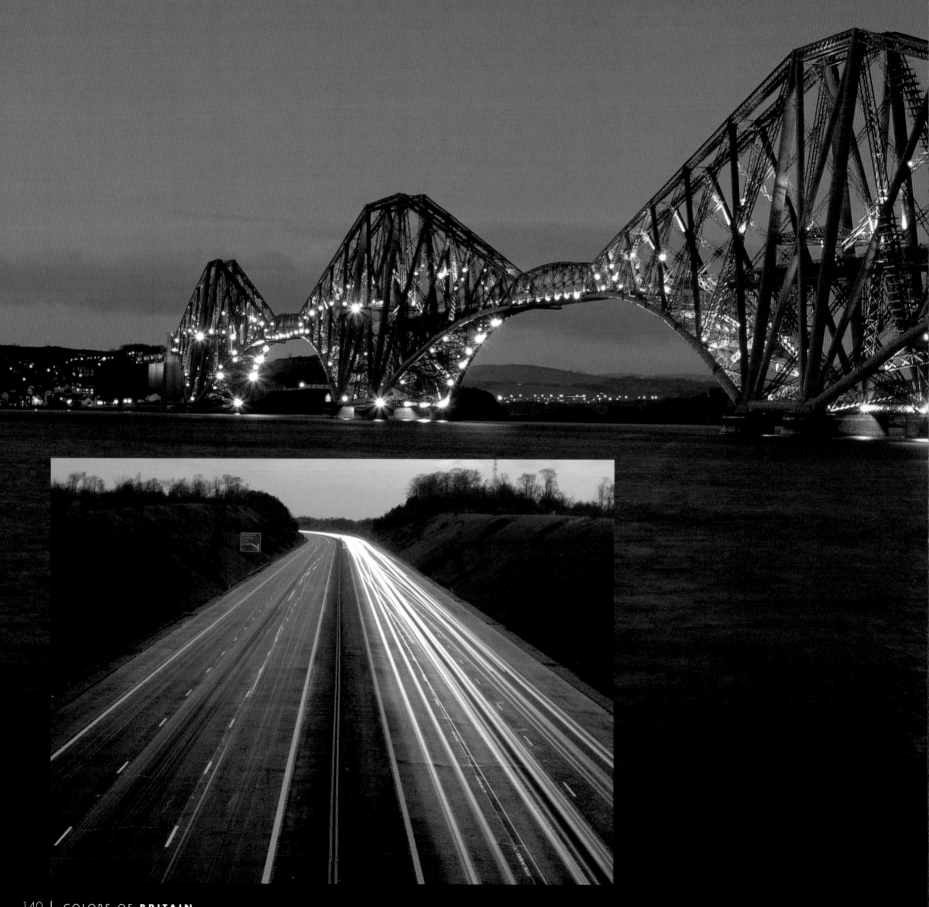

Prosperity leads us to generate more electricity than we need. So you'll often see the lights on after dark, and indeed some of the country's more prominent buildings floodlit.

The Firth of Forth railway bridge (above), a colossus of iron girders over 120 years old, looks positively ethereal with its own set of lights. Photographed at night from an overpass, using a long exposure, we gain a striking concept of a busy motorway (left).

Eastgate (above), in the heart of medieval Chester, is lit up as it could never have been when these timber-framed houses were first built. It's ten past four by the big clock—in the morning or the evening? It's hard to tell, but the shops look ready for action. Caernarfon Castle (above right), one of a line of 13th-century fortresses built by the English king Edward I to subdue Wales, was floodlit in 1969 to celebrate the investiture of Prince Charles as Prince of Wales. Edinburgh (top) is here brightened up by a show of fireworks during the city's annual arts festival.

After a clear, cold night, humidity is low, the atmosphere clean and transparent. With the sun low on the horizon, distant clouds glow pink, pale orange, and lemon, and nearer objects pick up the colors. So the Georgian windows and gray ashlar stonework of Attingham, Shropshire (above), borrow shades from a cold winter dawn. The mansion, centerpiece of Attingham Park near Shrewsbury, was built in the 1780s for the 1st Baron Berwick, incorporating a smaller Queen Anne house behind the colonnaded façade. In 1947 the 8th Lord Berwick bequeathed Attingham, its contents, and surrounding parkland to the heritage organization, the National Trust. Dawn spreads its magic over the swans on Rydall Water, in the Lake District (above).

CREDITS

The Automobile Association wishes to thank the following photo libraries for their assistance with this book.

www.britainonview.com 8, 10, 11t, 11b, 19bl, 26r, 28tc, 28bl, 28br, 29tl, 29tr, 29b, 31tc, 31bc, 48b, 107cl, 107cr, 107bc

Photodisc 137bl

Trademark of Transport for London 92r London Underground Roundel

The remaining photographs are held in the Association's own photo library (AA World Travel Library) and were taken by the following photographers:

Stuart Abrahams 100bl; Pat Aithie 139t, 139cr, 142br; Liz Allen 91br, 107t; Marius Alexander 52r, 60bc; Adrian Baker 24cr; Peter Baker Back cover cr, 3tcr, 4bl, 18br, 27, 37br, 41r, 52l, 92l, 93br, 101cr, 119t; Vic Bates 5br, 126br, 132cr, 132tr, 133; Jeff Beazley 85t; Andy Belcher 135bl; Pete Bennett 38l, 38tr; Malc Birkitt 37bl, 46l, 60tl, 67l, 71cl, 75b, 125; Edward Bowness 40b, 47t; Ian Burgum 114, 134tl, 134r; Michael Busselle 6, 22cr, 22b, 26l, 68r, 106bl; Jim Carnie 19bc, 31cr, 47b, 97; Chris Coe 84/5; Derek Croucher front cover main; Steve Day 5bl, 33t, 33b, 60tc, 61bc, 61br, 67tr, 71br, 73bc, 77, 78tl, 88t, 96t,

99t, 100br, 101cl, 110b, 127br, 136tr, 143r; Kenya Doran 61tc; Robert Eames 108bl, 110t; Jerry Edmanson 137br; Eric Ellington 30; Richard Elliott 135t, 138b, 140/1; Philip Enticknap 90br, 94; Derek Forss 19br, 34/5, 42l; Stephen Gibson 45l; Van Greaves 115l; Mike Hayward 138cr, 139cl; Anthony Hopkins 14; Nick Jenkins 109bl, 121; Caroline Jones 22tl, 22cl, 23tl, 23b, 66, 63tr, 66, 70bl, 93l, 101t, 105b, 109bc, 115r, 118b, 122l, 123, 142l, 143l; Max Jourdan 36bc, 42r, 43r, 62l, 83l, 90bl, 92t, 92r, 95l, 95r, 99b, 126bc, 130/1; Andrew Lawson 17, 21br, 38br, 46r, 54l, 56/7, 76/7, 136br; Cameron Lees 106c; Tom Mackie 5bcr, 21tl, 24tl, 50/1, 61tr, 72bc, 74b, 78/9, 98/9, 108bc, 111, 116, 117, 127bl, 129r, 137t; S&O Mathews 21tr, 31l, 70cr, 71tr, 71bl, 122b; Simon McBride 53l, 83r, 138t; Jenny McMillan back cover cl, 3tcl, 87cr, 87cl, 95c; John Miller 12/3, 36br, 44r, 54br, 62b, 72bl, 75t, 91bl, 101c, 101br, 132l, 144; Roger Moss 9, 21bl, 25cl, 67br, 78tr, 80tr, 100tl, 100tr, 106tr; Ken Paterson 22tr, 23c, 55br, 68l, 70bc, 90br, 96b, 103c, 122tr, 128l; Clive Sawyer 32r; Barrie Smith 48t, 73bl, 86/7, 87t; Jonathan Smith 60br, 61tl, 61bl, 102l, 102c, 102r, 103r; Tony Souter 32c, 44l, 48c, 71tc, 136bl; Jon Sparks 15; Rick Strange 4bc, 36bl, 39, 53r, 69b, 93bc, 138cl; David Tarn back cover r, 3tr; Michael Taylor 72br, 82; Rupert Tenison 63tl, 106cl; James Tims 69t, 93tr, 127bc,

140b; Peter Trenchard 45r; Andy Tryner 41l, 120; Richard Turpin 105t; Wyn Voysey 32l, 49r, 80tl, 80b, 100c, 128r; Ronnie Weir 37bc, 49l, 109br, 124; Stephen Whitehorne 16, 23cr, 62r, 81, 108br, 112/3, 118t, 119b; Linda Whitwam 18bl, 18bc, 20, 24b, 25tl, 25r, 54bc, 58, 59, 60tr, 60bl, 135br; Harry Williams 74t, 136tl; Tim Woodcock 4br, 55bl, 64l, 64r, 65tl, 65bl, 126bl, 129l; Gregory Wrona back cover l, 3tl; Jon Wyand 40t.